How to Use Primary Sources

HOW TO
USE PRIMARY SOURCES

Helen H. Carey
Judith E. Greenberg

A GROLIER COMPANY

A Social Studies Skills Book
FRANKLIN WATTS / 1983
New York / London / Toronto / Sydney

Photographs and illustrations courtesy of
Helen H. Carey: p. 6; Judith E. Greenberg: p. 22;
National Archives: pp. 25, 26, 40, 41, 44, 46, 47;
Montgomery County Historical Society: pp. 37, 38;
Ginger Giles: pp. 5, 13, 16, 29, 32, 36, 50, 62, 65.

Excerpt from Hoflund Diary courtesy of
Winifred Harvey, Adelphi, Md.
Excerpt from Wigodsky Diary courtesy of
Ronn Karp, Potomac, Md.

Library of Congress Cataloging in Publication Data

Carey, Helen H.
How to use primary sources.

(A Social studies skills book)
Bibliography: p.
Includes index.
Summary: Describes how to use documents, diaries
and journals, people, art, museums, historic sites,
and other places as direct sources of information.
1. History—Research—Juvenile literature.
2. History—Sources—Juvenile literature.
[1. History—Research.   2. History—Sources.   3. Research]
I. Greenberg, Judith E.   II. Title. III. Series.
D16.C247 1983   907'.2   83-10199
ISBN 0-531-04674-5

Contents

To our mothers
Ruth E. Holleran
Rosalind Schlossberg

How to Use Primary Sources

Introduction

Diaries, letters, photographs, lockets, dinosaurs, and mummies—these are called *primary sources.* They are direct sources of information that tell us about people, places, and events. Primary sources include firsthand reports, on-the-spot sketches, and even articles of clothing and jewelry.

This book will help you understand what primary sources are and how to use them in school projects and reports. Primary sources are not substitutes for the kind of material that can only be found by doing research in the library. But primary sources can supplement your basic research in many ways. Here are some of the primary sources that will be discussed:

- Interviews and oral accounts
- Photographs, paintings, and statues
- Objects used in the past, such as tools, dishes, and clothing
- Legal documents (such as marriage certificates and census records)
- Letters
- Diaries and journals
- Contents of museums, historic sites, and historic societies

Questions such as What are primary sources? How can they help me learn the truth? are answered in the first chapter. Two fascinating case studies illustrate how primary sources can lead to important discoveries.

In chapter 2 you will learn that people are good primary sources of information. This chapter teaches you how to prepare and conduct a successful interview and include what you have learned in oral and written reports.

Chapter 3 explains how to interpret works of art, such as paintings, photographs, monuments, and statues. You will learn how to view pieces for their overall beauty and to look at them closely for details.

Chapters 4 and 5 discuss written accounts as primary sources of information. Chapter 4 covers a variety of legal documents and records, while chapter 5 deals with diaries and journals. You will learn how to get the most out of written accounts by categorizing information, making generalizations that are supported by facts, and inferring information not directly stated.

In chapter 6 you will read about ways to bring back information from museums and historic sites, and how to present your newly acquired information in a paper or speech. You will find tips for good note-taking, being selective, and summarizing.

Who uses primary sources besides students? Chapter 7 looks at various careers in which primary sources play a major role.

Using primary sources is an exciting way to learn. You will use them throughout your school years and after you graduate, and this book will get you started.

1

Primary Sources: What Are They?

In the quiet time that follows a family reunion such as a Thanksgiving feast, someone is likely to remember a story about the family. Telling the story will trigger other stories.

"Do you remember the Thanksgiving three years ago when Aunt Mildred put the leftover turkey outside on the porch steps and a dog ran off with all of next day's dinner?"

"Oh, yeah, that was funny. Uncle Clarence chased that dog all over creation. And remember. . ."

Aunt Mildred, Uncle Clarence, and all the other people who witnessed the "great turkey robbery" are original, or primary, sources of information. They can tell you the true story because they were there when it happened. Any questions you might have can be answered by going directly to them.

It probably won't surprise you to discover that there is often disagreement over some of the details in these stories. And when the stories concern events of long ago, people's memories fade. Where do you turn if you want to find out what really happened when one relative recalls one thing, and another relative recalls something entirely different?

In order to get the facts, you may have to try to find as many original sources as you can. If there are no longer any witnesses alive, you may have to turn to other primary sources for the information you are seeking, such as old newspapers, photographs, and diaries.

Often it is very important to learn the truth about matters that happened in the past. For example, suppose a bank is looking for the relatives of someone who deposited $1 million in 1900 and never came back again. The bank now wants to close the account and give the money to the person's closest relatives, but the heirs must prove that they are related. Can you imagine the mad scramble there would be for birth records, old letters, wills, and other legal papers?

Researching primary sources to learn the truth can be easy or a long and difficult process. You will read about how one expert spent years trying to discover the true cause of Napoleon Bonaparte's death. But first, let's look at how primary sources were able to provide a new headstone on the grave of a Civil War veteran.

THE CASE OF
THE MISSING GRAVE MARKER

Three years after his headstone was reported missing, relatives of Private John McKibben gave up trying to recover the missing marker and applied to the Veterans' Adminstration (VA) for a replacement. The VA would replace old or damaged grave markers of veterans if it could be proved that the individual had in fact served in the armed forces.

The family members looked first in the old family Bible for McKibben's dates of birth and death. Why an old Bible? Because most states did not begin keeping vital statistics (birth and death dates and other impor-

Before states began keeping vital statistics, birth and death dates were often recorded in the family Bible.

Clarion, Pa. Aug 12. 1892

John McKibben Esq
McDonald Pa

Dear Sir & Comrade:

your affidavit relating to the march does not agree
with mine, if you recollect we were marching
from Warrenton over the Warrenton pike when we
were suddenly stopped by the enemy being in our
rear, and fired into us, it is the place where Henry
Wetten lost his leg, it was then we march around
and came to Manassa or Bull run, it was rough
and dark, that is my recollection, the next
morning I told you to go and get a sick
ticket, you have the names of places mixed, or I
have
                    Respectfully
                        W. A. Sipler

*This letter, written in 1892, confirmed that
Private John McKibben served in the armed forces.*

tant information) until 1900. Before this time it was up to the family to keep track of when family members were born and when they died. Most families kept these names and dates in the book that was most likely to be handed down to the next generation—the Bible.

The McKibben family Bible provided the date of Private John McKibben's death. This discovery made it very easy to locate the back issue of the local newspaper that contained his death notice. Near the bottom of the account was the important sentence: "Mr. John McKibben served as a private in Company H, Fifth Pennsylvania, from 1862 to 1865."

The VA, like most official agencies, accepts newspaper notices as primary sources because newspapers are a record of the day. But in case further proof was required, the McKibben family produced additional evidence from the contents of an old trunk. They found the soldier's blue uniform (moth-eaten, but largely intact), and a letter from a former army buddy who was with Private McKibben at the battle of Bull Run. (See page 5.) Apparently it was written in answer to a question McKibben had asked about the battle many years later.

Gathering evidence on whether or not Private McKibben served in the army in the Civil War was fairly simple because so many primary sources could be located. These included the handwritten letter, his uniform, and the notice in the newspaper. All these materials helped to place a new headstone on the grave of Private John McKibben (1835–1910) in time for Veterans Day 1983.

THE CASE OF
THE POISONED EMPEROR

Is it possible to investigate a death that occurred over 160 years ago? Using primary sources, a Swedish dentist, Sven Forshufvud, investigated the death of Napoleon Bonaparte, suspecting that it was caused by arsenic poisoning. Was it murder? Sven Forshufvud set out to prove that it was.

Forshufvud was more than a dentist. He was a scientist who did research in biology with a special interest in toxicology (the study of poisons). Dentistry, biology, and toxicology were his vocations (career); his avocation (hobby or special interest) was the life of Napoleon Bonaparte, the emperor of France from 1804 to 1815. Because of this lifelong interest, the dentist's home was filled with objects and pictures relating to Napoleon. He read books and anything else that he could find about Napoleon. He was especially interested in the theories about Napoleon's death: no one could agree on the exact cause. It remained a mystery why an apparently healthy man weakened and died. In 1955 Forshufvud read a newly published book about Napoleon's last days.

The book contained the memoirs of Louis Marchand, Napoleon's servant and companion. The memoirs gave a firsthand account of Napoleon's life on St. Helena, where he died in exile. The daily log Marchand kept noted the changes in Napoleon's health and described the symptoms of illnesses Napoleon experienced. As Forshufvud read each account, he began to suspect that the symptoms described were those of long-term arsenic poisoning. That Napoleon had died of arsenic poisoning was so obvious to Forshufvud, he thought it must be equally obvious to others. But that was not the case.

For the next four years Forshufvud read other articles and books about the Marchand memoirs, but not one mentioned arsenic poisoning. He realized that he had to investigate and prove the theory on his own. He started by gathering all the primary sources he could find that were associated with Napoleon's life on St. Helena. He already had read the memoirs of others on the island with Napoleon at the time of his death. He began,

[8]

however, by studying the autopsy report, Marchand's memoirs, and the notes of Napoleon's doctor. With these sources he was able to make a time line (a chart that places events in chronological order) showing what symptoms had appeared and when. This time line showed how the suspected poisoning took place over a lengthy period. But more evidence was needed.

To get this evidence, Forshufvud turned to Hamilton Smith, a Scottish toxicologist. Forshufvud had read an article by Smith in a chemistry journal about his new method for testing for arsenic poisoning. This method required only a single strand of hair, while other tests required a greater amount. Toxicologists had known for a long time that traces of arsenic always remain in hair. Forshufvud wondered if he could find a piece of Napoleon's hair.

Strands of hair were popular keepsakes in Napoleon's time and he had given many locks of his hair as souvenirs. Also, when he died, his hair was cut off and saved. Forshufvud hoped that collectors would be willing to give up a few strands for testing by the new method. Later, Smith improved the test so that small sections of the same piece of hair could be tested to show the amount of arsenic taken over a period of time. These primary sources—just a few hairs—perhaps could reveal the truth about Napoleon's death.

The first strand of hair was supplied by a French expert on Napoleon. The hair was tested for arsenic and found to contain large amounts. Having the needed evidence, Forshufvud published his theory.

At first many scholars rejected Forshufvud's theory. But two experts—one from Switzerland and the other from Australia—were eager to test the new idea. Both sent strands of Napoleon's hair for testing, which were tested by Smith's improved method. The results definitely showed arsenic poisoning over a period of time and were compared to the time line of symptoms. The results

[9]

and symptoms corresponded, and the theory gained wider acceptance.

By conducting other tests, Forshufvud found that Napoleon had been given two medicines widely used at the time. Used alone, they were not harmful, but combined with the arsenic, the mixture was deadly. Forshufvud surmised that whoever poisoned Napoleon guessed correctly that these medicines would be prescribed, and that person caused his death by adding arsenic.

The body of Napoleon, when moved from St. Helena to France for final burial about twenty years after his death, supplied more evidence. When the body was uncovered, it showed no decomposition, and it had been in the ground for years! The arsenic in Napoleon's system, given over a period of time, had acted to preserve the body. Forshufvud was positive. Napoleon had been poisoned.

The next question was Who did it? Some research about the lives of those on the island helped to reveal the poisoner. A strand of hair showed that the deliberate poisoning started before 1818. (Napoleon died in 1821.) People who came to the island after 1818 were removed from the list of suspects. The person had to have had access to the food and drink Napoleon consumed and had to have been considered a trusted friend. These criteria narrowed the possibilities. Researching in depth the lives of the suspects, Forshufvud finally decided that Charles Montholon, a French aristocrat in charge of Napoleon's household, was his probable poisoner.

Always keep an open mind when gathering information from primary sources. Sometimes new and important evidence is uncovered that will cause you to change your mind. Forshufvud himself may have to reevaluate his theory in light of new evidence from a recent reanalysis of Napoleon's hair. Modern, more sophisticated analyses have revealed that the hair contained moderately high levels of antimony, used in many nineteenth-century medicines, and not arsenic. These scientists believe that if Napoleon did have any arsenic in his system, it probably came from the wallpaper in his home, also recently tested as a primary source and found to have been painted with a green pigment containing arsenic. The vapors from this common nineteenth-century pigment could cause weakness, nausea, and enlarged limbs, symptoms that Napoleon suffered. Napoleon may have died from stomach cancer and not arsenic poisoning.

DRAWING CONCLUSIONS FROM PRIMARY SOURCES

Primary sources reveal the true story. No one has "interpreted" the facts, added something, or left something out. Interpreting the information you get from primary sources is up to you. You must draw your own conclusions. Uncovering information that has been previously overlooked can lead to a new viewpoint about an event, or a new theory. Forshufvud felt he uncovered a murder by using primary sources. But new evidence suggests Napoleon died of stomach cancer. While you probably won't solve a mystery, it is possible for you to draw important conclusions that will enrich your school projects and reports.

The first step is to make sure you are clear in your mind what you want to find out. Then, once your purpose is clear, you have to decide where to look for the information you are seeking. The McKibben family, for example, looked in an old newspaper for the information they needed. And Forshufvud used the test for arsenic poisoning as well as a record of the actual symptoms Napoleon exhibited.

For some of your reports the facts you have learned through your reading may be enough. But to cover other subjects adequately, you may need to supplement what you already know with material from other sources.

Suppose, for example, that you want to write a report about how Americans at home helped in the war effort during World War II. From your reading you find out that women, children, teen-agers, and the men who worked in essential industries all contributed to the war effort. But unless you have some specific details to use as examples, your report will contain nothing more than hazy ideas. You might be able to say that for the first time large numbers of women worked outside the home, people bought war bonds, and young people did their part by working on farms instead of going on vacations. You might also be able to tell that the government started a system of rationing food and other items that were in short supply, but you may not know any details. With material as general as this, you cannot write a very interesting report, let alone draw any conclusions from the information you have collected.

Suppose that instead of relying on reading material, you interview family members and friends who lived during the war. These primary sources will surely be able to recall specific instances in which they or people they knew worked in factories, bought savings stamps and war bonds, collected rubber and scrap metal, worked on farms, or took courses in home nursing and first aid. Some of these sources may be able to let you see a war ration book. Every American had one of these books during the war and many families have kept them as souvenirs. The ration stamps were used whenever families bought meat, sugar, shoes, or tires. From the list of these items that were rationed, you might be able to draw some conclusions about why each family could buy only certain amounts of food and other items and about the way the rationing system worked.

Family members and friends who lived during World War II are excellent sources of information about that time.

As you gather your material about the home front from interviews, other sources of information might be suggested to you. Newspapers, letters, diaries, and pictures are good primary sources. With enough facts, ideas, descriptive details, examples, and incidents, you will be able to carry out your purpose of explaining how important the activities at home were to the total war effort.

But what if you want to convince others that the war effort changed the attitude toward working women in America? Then you must evaluate all the data you have collected, keeping only the information on women working in industries and in the armed forces, and set the rest aside. When you have enough facts, you can proceed to the next step of writing your report. If important facts are still missing, or you have facts that contradict your conclusion, then you must find more materials that do suit your purpose. Remember, it's always a good idea to test each piece of material before using it in your report. Ask yourself, Will this information help others understand what I'm trying to say? If the example, incident, or detail contributes to your stated purpose, you should plan to include it in your report; if it does not, you should leave it out, no matter how interesting it may be.

2

People as Primary Sources

Martha and Paul were planning to prepare oral reports on the same subject—submarine warfare in World War II. Since both were interested in the subject, both felt they could produce good reports for their history projects. But what a difference between the two reports!

Paul was not sure about the size, appearance, and living conditions aboard submarines. He knew there were cramped quarters for sleeping, eating, and working, and that they were probably not satisfactory, but he was not very clear on why they weren't. He was not able to present any details about how it felt to be in a submarine during warfare, or how it felt to be under the ocean, or in a battle. His report showed a lack of preparation, and even though he was the best speaker in the class, he could not give a good talk with this kind of sketchy material.

Martha, on the other hand, was able to relate specific details about the heat and poor air in a submerged submarine, the feelings of being closed in while under the ocean, the average distance a sub can travel under the ocean on battery power, the organization of the various compartments in the submarine, the duties of the officers and the crew, and the hazards of submarine duty during wartime. With the type of material Martha had col-

lected, she was able to give a very interesting talk, even though she felt she was not as confident a speaker as Paul.

Where did Martha get the samples she used in her report? Unlike Paul, she planned her report well ahead of time, and she included with the material from her reading specific details she had gotten from an interview with her uncle. Since her uncle had served on a submarine in World War II he became an excellent primary source for her history report. Let's see how.

To complete her report, Martha went to the library where she found a lot of material about how submarines were used during World War II and how they looked. But she wanted to know what it had been like to actually live on a submarine. She learned from her family that her uncle had served on a submarine during the war. She decided to interview him for the details she needed.

Interviewing people may look easy on television, but a lot of work precedes the actual meeting. If you come to your interview well prepared, it should proceed smoothly. Martha prepared for her interview by following the steps listed below.

To conduct my interview I need to

1. decide on my source, ask the person for an interview, and set a date, time, and place for the meeting;

Martha's uncle provided her with fascinating details and anecdotes about life on a submarine during World War II.

2. do background research so I will be familiar with the material to be discussed and be able to understand the terms used;

3. make a list of the questions I want to ask;

4. decide if I will use a tape recorder or take notes; make sure my tape recorder is in working order;

5. practice asking my questions;

6. review my background notes and questions and delete any questions that are repetitious;

7. prepare an introduction that will explain to the interviewee the purpose of the interview and how it will be used;

8. check my materials one more time right before the actual interview takes place.

If you are going to inteview your own uncle, for example, you probably won't be nervous. But interviews with those outside the family might be easier if you practice with a friend or classmate. Interview a friend about school or a hobby. Follow the steps shown in the checklist and tape this pretend interview. Replay the interview and evaluate your questions and interviewing skills. Make the necessary changes before you conduct the actual interview.

Martha prepared approximately fifteen to twenty questions to ask her uncle. Her first questions concerned the basic facts:

- How long did you serve on board a submarine?

- Does everyone in the Navy serve on a sub? If not, how do you get picked for sub duty?

- Where did your sub travel? How long were you in these places?

- How big are the working, eating, and sleeping spaces on a sub?

She next asked about his experiences during submarine duty:

- How does it feel to be under the ocean? Are you aware of the depth?
- Did you ever feel trapped or closed in on the sub?
- How are battle conditions on a sub different from other naval battles?
- Would you recommend submarine service to others?
- What was the scariest experience you had? The funniest? The strangest?
- Did your family worry about you because you were on a submarine?
- Is there anything else you can tell me about life aboard a submarine in World War II?

EVALUATING INTERVIEWS

Consider these five questions when you evaluate information from an interview:

1. How qualified is the person you interviewed to answer your questions? (If Martha's uncle had served on a submarine for only one month, he could not be cited as an expert on submarine living conditions.)

2. Is the person giving statements of fact or opinion? Both are important, but you should recognize that they are different.

3. Is this information important? How necessary is it to my report? Learning what to put in your report and what to leave out involves making decisions. If

the information answers one of your questions, include it in your report.

4. Will my audience be informed or merely entertained by the information I have collected? Be sure to include important information, but an amusing anecdote or exciting incident will add color to your report.

When you interview, remember that there are at least two sides to every issue. Fairness as well as truth require you to give the other side equal time. If your interview, for example, was intended to "prove" that submarine duty was the most hazardous of all wartime duty, you may have to compare it to the duties of pilots and infantrymen. After you have compared the hazards of each job, you may want to leave the decision to your audience. Giving both sides does not diminish your own claims; in fact, it sometimes makes them stronger.

Follow up your interview with letters or calls thanking people for their time.

Martha must now put this information into her report. Since hers is to be an oral report, Martha can explain the interview and either replay parts of the tape, read direct quotes to the class, or summarize the most interesting and useful facts.

In a written report, Martha would have to explain what her sources were for the material she includes, and tell which information was from the interview and which from books and other material. She would have to be careful to present the material so that readers understood which were factual statements and which were her uncle's opinions.

Other materials you might include in your report, either oral or written, depend on the type of report it is and its length. You start by thinking back over the material you have collected. For example, Martha might put the people and events from her uncle's firsthand account into chronological order so that all the details are included and the audience gets a clear picture of the experience.

Martha might decide to begin her presentation with an explanation of her primary source—in her case, her uncle—to establish the reliability of her information. She could present, for example, a brief family tree as a way of documenting that her uncle was the correct age to have fought in the war. She should include only the information on the family tree that has a bearing on the point of her topic. (For instance, the fact that her uncle's second and third cousins were too young to serve in the war would be irrelevant.)

Visuals such as family trees are good ways to present information from primary sources. What is important is that you take the time to think about ways to make your material fulfill your purpose. If these visual aids help you to tie together your facts, descriptions, examples, and incidents so that you can produce a good, clear report, then be sure to include them with the material acquired from interviews.

*Old photographs, such as this
one taken around 1915, can tell you
a lot about life in the past.*

3

Art and Other Sources

Paintings, photographs, cartoons, posters, statues, and models sometimes can tell you more about certain topics than words. But you must examine these visual aids closely in order to learn anything meaningful from them.

IDENTIFYING CENTRAL ISSUES

There are all kinds of visual primary sources, from paintings to statues to models, and as you study them you must ask such questions as: What is all this about? What am I supposed to be thinking when I see this? What is the main problem or purpose? Does this apply to my project or report?

All forms of visuals can tell a story, give facts, show how something works, and reveal how people looked in the past. The personal photograph on page 22, for example, reveals many things about the time in which these two women lived. You can conclude from this picture that the women knew each other, and that they were probably close friends or relatives because one has her arm around the other. The hairstyles and clothing indicate that the picture was taken around 1915.

To get any meaning from these primary sources you must sharpen your reading and interpreting skills. Let us see how you can develop these skills by looking at page 25 and reading the poster widely distributed during World War I (1914–1918).

1. Skim for an overall impression of the message in the poster.
2. List the people and main objects in the poster.
3. Read the words carefully and combine them with the pictures to identify the purpose of the poster.
4. Finally, infer or interpret the meaning of the words and pictures. Women did their part during World War I. They helped by nursing the wounded and acting as guards. Even though they didn't fight on the battlefields, women loved their country, too, and did their part.

As you develop your skill in reading this type of visual material, you will be able to identify useful information and grasp the main idea. Then you can check the material for accuracy with what you have learned from your other sources of information.

PHOTOGRAPHS, PAINTINGS, DRAWINGS, AND STATUES

Sometimes pictures can effectively and dramatically convey concepts. Let us consider the concept of "separate but equal" schools for blacks and whites. In the past, many people believed that even though black children

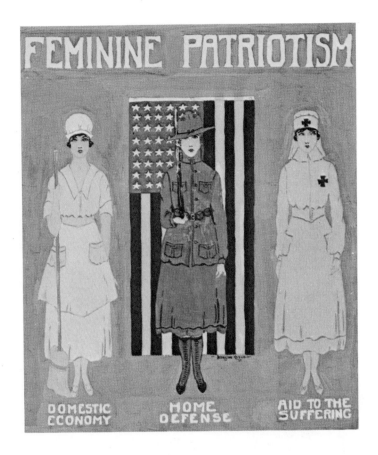

*This poster tells something of the
role of women during World War I.*

went to their own schools their education would be as good as the education white children received. But what questions do the pictures on this page raise about the quality of black schools under the separate-but-equal idea? How do you think the two schools compare, based on what is shown in the photographs? What obvious differences between the two schools can you find?

Photography was not invented until the 1800s, so you will not be able to find any photographs from the Revolutionary War or earlier. But there are drawings, paintings, diagrams and statues available. By looking closely at these visual representations, you can learn a great deal of important information. The statue of the Minute Man in Concord, Massachusetts, for example, continues to stir the imaginations of Americans although the Revolutionary War has been over for more than two hundred years.

For example, those who view the statue see a young man standing ready to fight for the right to be free. The fact that he is not wearing a uniform shows that he belonged to a peace-loving nation. The plow represents farming, the major occupation of that time. The statue expresses the independent spirit of the American people.

Statues like the Minute Man are similar to the Lincoln Memorial or the statues of George Washington and Thomas Jefferson in Washington, D.C. The Minute Man memorializes all the brave farmers who successful-

The public school for white children (above) and for black children (below) in Macon County, Georgia, in 1936.

ly fought the British soldiers at Concord Bridge in 1775. As a primary source it conveys a feeling of the spirit of the time.

INTERPRETING
WORKS OF ART

There are several things to keep in mind when you use pieces of art as primary sources.

First, who is the artist? Why did he or she want to show this scene in particular? How accurately do the statue or the figures in a painting show reality? Many artists distort reality to achieve a particular effect.

Paul Revere's engraving of the Boston Massacre, which may have been a copy of a picture by artist Harry Pelham, showed more colonists killed than there actually were in order to arouse his fellow colonists against the British. Viewers of Revere's engraving must consider the artist's bias and inaccuracies. Once these are accounted for, the engraving becomes a useful eyewitness source of information.

Revere also drew a diagram of the Boston Massacre, which was used at the trial of the British soldiers in 1770. In the diagram, however, he drew the true number of Americans being killed—five—instead of the seven he showed in his painting. His diagram was used as a primary source in the trial. Why do you think he was more accurate in the drawing he prepared for the court? How

Statues can convey a sense of the personalities of important historical figures.

[28]

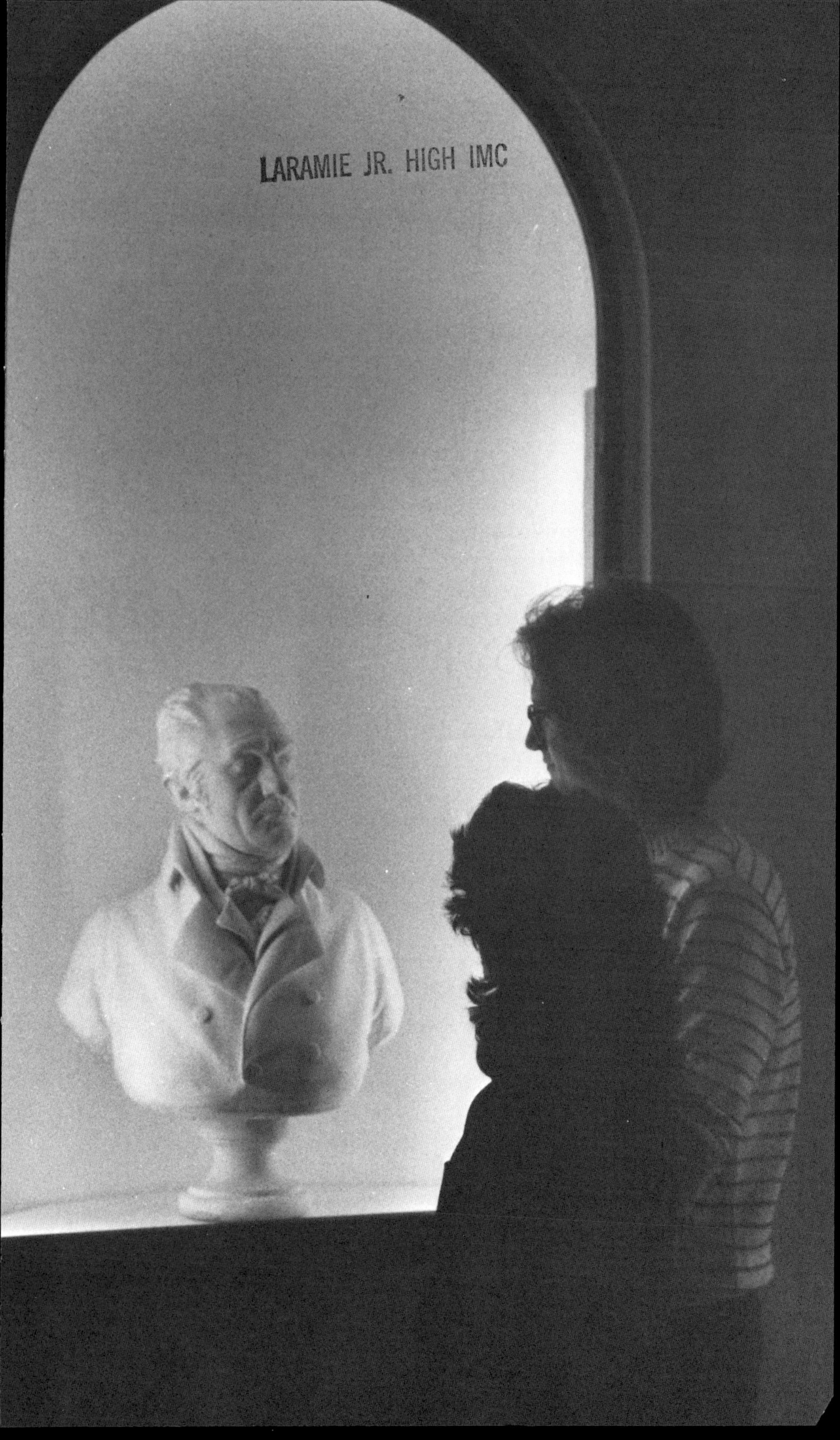

do you think historians regard the diagram as compared to the painting of the Boston Massacre?

The second factor to consider is how much background information you have. In order to get the most out of a painting, picture, or statue, you must know something about it. Reading about Lincoln before you visit the Lincoln Memorial will make viewing the statue much more memorable and give you an opportunity to better evaluate the image and its message.

Thirdly, in analyzing a work of art you should be able to identify the details. Composition, or the arrangement of elements, is important. Divide the painting into four sections. Look carefully at one section at a time, noting as many details as you can in each section until you have covered the entire picture. Then consider all the details. You may end up with a totally different impression than the one you had when you first looked at the painting.

THREE-DIMENSIONAL
PRIMARY SOURCES

Statues and models of real objects such as sailing ships have one big advantage over photographs and paintings as primary sources of information. They have the extra dimension of depth. The third dimension of depth (relief) helps you see more details. There is a problem, though, that you must consider when using statues and models as sources of information. You must pay attention to scale.

Scale

Carved on Mount Rushmore are the faces of four great Americans. These heads of George Washington, Thomas

Jefferson, Abraham Lincoln, and Theodore Roosevelt are among the largest figures ever made. The memorial is taller than the Great Pyramid in Egypt and took fourteen years to complete. Each head is about 60 feet (18 m) tall. That is as high as a five-story building! If the faces were attached to bodies, each man would be approximately 465 feet (142 m) tall.

In order to carve the faces in the correct proportion, the sculptor, Gutzon Borglum, and his staff used models of noses, ears, and foreheads on the scale of 1 inch to the foot. The faces were then cut with drills and dynamite. Gutzon did not live long enough to see his lifework completed. He died in 1941 and his son, James Lincoln, finished the statues that same year.

Model-makers and sculptors get the facts about their subjects from other primary sources: photographs (if available), people who knew the subject, and from as many other sources as they can find. By working this way, they can be as accurate as possible.

Next, they decide on the best scale to use. Using too large a scale may mean that the finished model or statue will be too big to fit into the place it is designed for. Too small a scale may mean that some details will have to be left out.

Now that you have some idea why models and statues differ—in size, in the details included, and in what is to be shown—you can understand why it is important to find out what scale has been used.

The best way to find out what scale has been used is to turn to the object itself. Models of sailing ships, trains, and Conestoga wagons usually have the scale used printed on the base of the display. If the scale says 1/4 inch = 1 foot, you should have no trouble figuring out how big the real object is. The scale of a statue may be harder to find, but calls to the park service or historical society will usually provide you with information.

*Models are accurate representations
of historical objects.*

MAKING
YOUR OWN MODELS

There will be many occasions when you will want to
make a model as part of a project. The scale you use for
your models should be determined by their intended use.
If you want your Conestoga wagon to be shown against a
background of western countryside and an Indian attack,

you will have to consider these proportions in deciding what scale to make the wagon.

In the construction and use of models and other three-dimensional objects

1. keep your purpose clearly in mind;

2. present the information accurately; don't try to create an artistic masterpiece;

3. plan ahead of time what details, such as lettering, people, and objects, you will be showing in your model. These details have a bearing on the scale you will use;

4. try to visualize the real object the model represents;

5. figure out what materials you will need to make your model and how much the materials will cost;

6. estimate the time it will take you to make your model. If it is going to take too long, consider whether the knowledge you have gained in doing the research would be better used in another form of illustration.

HOW TO USE VISUALS
IN WRITTEN AND ORAL REPORTS

Paintings, pictures, artifacts, and models are easy to use in reports, especially in oral reports. There is less of a problem of What should I say? because these visuals help you to tell your story. For example, suppose the topic you have chosen to report on is "Life on the Frontier." If you select your visuals carefully you will be able to make the point that people used building materials that were available where they lived. And your models or pictures will illustrate why log cabins were the best solution to the problem of shelter in wooded areas, sod houses were used on treeless plains, and teepees made of skins were useful for temporary Indian settlements.

Once you have decided what visuals to use, the next thing to do is become thoroughly familiar with your topic. Try to know more about these homes than anyone else in your group. For this reason, you should collect information from several sources. You should not glance hurriedly at a picture or drawing, jot down a few notes, and rush off to make your model or diagram. This kind of preparation will result in your giving a poor talk. Take the time to gather plenty of details.

The wording for your talk can be either written out in full, or in an outline. Either way, be sure to use a logical order for your material. Order is to your talk what a map is to a person taking a trip; both show where you are going.

One other point is important. The information you are presenting must be accurate, so be sure to tell where you got your material; give your references. You should also offer your conclusions at the end of your report. How well suited were these early homes to the environment and living conditions at the time? What were their good features? What were the disadvantages? Could anything better have been invented?

Finally, be prepared to hand in a written report along with the pictures or models used in your oral report when your presentation is over. Your teacher may want to make suggestions for improvement.

Occasions to use visuals in written reports are many. Visuals such as pictures, diagrams, drawings, and photographs are effective ways to inform. They can be used to illustrate such topics as historic or new inventions, the solar system, stockades and forts, Viking ships and ships used by Columbus, airplanes and rockets, and styles of clothing over the years. Most of the hints offered in using visuals in oral reports are useful for written reports.

4

Documents

Documents particularly useful as primary sources are official papers containing laws, court decisions, treaties, and statements about government actions and policies. Policymaking government documents can be found in places such as the National Archives in Washington, D.C. This important repository contains the primary documents of our nation, including the original Constitution of the United States and the Declaration of Independence. In these documents you can read exactly what was said by the founders of our country. Other important primary sources are newspapers, telegrams, census reports, letters, and maps.

WHAT CAN YOU LEARN
FROM DOCUMENTS?

Original sources tell us about the lives of important people and events. Before you try to use a document, ask yourself these questions:

- What kind of document is it? Is it a legal paper, newspaper, policy report, letter, or telegram?

[35]

Documents can tell you about laws, court decisions, treaties, and government policies.

- When was the document written and what was happening in the world?
- Who is mentioned in the document?
- What effect did the document have?
- Can I use this document as a primary source?
- How can I present the information? Should it be in a written report? Oral report? Or can I present the information on a chart, on slides, in a graph, or as a survey?

Marriage Certificate

Even a document as ordinary as a marriage certificate can add information to a report or presentation. This certificate, for example, is dated 1893 and might be useful for someone researching his or her family history. Perhaps you are interested in a section of land and this document proves that a church by the name of St. Rose once stood on that particular spot. Or, it shows that the state of Maryland kept records of marriages one hundred years ago.

Notice the small print in the lower left-hand corner. The marriage license is a contract between two people, and a copy of the certificate was to be given to the two contracting parties. Do you find it surprising that such a statement appeared long before the recent women's liberation movement?

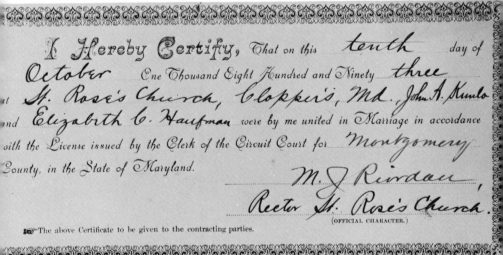

I Hereby Certify, That on this tenth day of October One Thousand Eight Hundred and Ninety three at St. Rose's Church, Clopper's, Md., John A. Kunlo and Elizabeth C. Haufman were by me united in Marriage in accordance with the License issued by the Clerk of the Circuit Court for Montgomery County, in the State of Maryland.

M. J. Riordan,
Rector St. Rose's Church.
(OFFICIAL CHARACTER.)

☞ The above Certificate to be given to the contracting parties.

A marriage certificate from 1893

[37]

Stock Certificate

The owner of this certificate owned ten shares of stock in the Washington and Rockville Turnpike in 1852. Today the "turnpike" is called Rockville Pike and has four lanes of traffic in each direction! What has happened to the road since 1852? Is the company that built the road from the money raised by selling stock still in existence? What happened to the stock's value over the years? This certificate was issued for ten shares and cost a total of $200. How much was each share worth at the time? Notice the

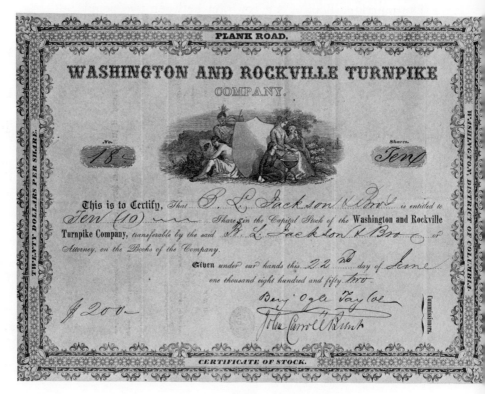

A stock certificate dated 1852

words at the top of the certificate. What do you think a "plank road" was? Why might it have been important to put these words on the certificate?

This certificate is also a clue to the nature of the transportation system in the United States during the 1800s. What type of vehicle do you think would be traveling on a plank (wooden) road? Who might be expected to use this road? You can't find all the answers to these and other questions from this stock certificate, but this document could lead you to an old map of the area and launch you on a study of the history of Rockville. In other words, this primary source could be just one in a series of sources you might find.

The Zimmerman Telegram

An exciting example of a primary-source document is the World War I telegram in which the German Foreign Minister, Arthur Zimmermann, offered its former territory in Texas, New Mexico, and Arizona to Mexico if it would join the German side. This telegram, sent in 1917, aroused public opinion to such a degree that the United States probably declared war against Germany sooner than it would have.

To keep America from finding out about the secret proposal, the Germans sent the telegram in code. The British intercepted the telegram and forwarded it to President Wilson. Wilson had been reelected partly because of his pledge to keep America out of the war in Europe. This single document so angered the American people that they wanted to declare war.

The actual telegram and decoded translation appear on pages 40 and 41.

Certain facts become clear from reading the Zimmermann telegram:

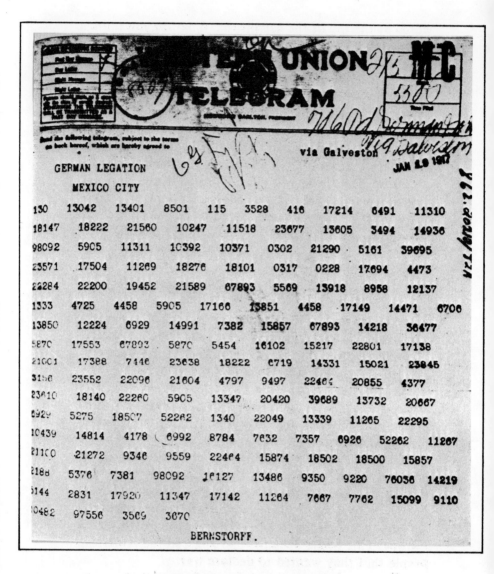

*The Zimmermann telegram
and translation, offering
United States land to
Mexico if it would join the
German side in World War I.*

FROM 2nd from London # 5747.

"We intend to begin on the first of February
unrestricted submarine warfare. We shall endeavor
in spite of this to keep the United States of
America neutral. In the event of this not succeed-
ing, we make Mexico a proposal of alliance on the
following basis: make war together, make peace
together, generous financial support and an understanding on our part that Mexico is to reconquer
the lost territory in Texas, New Mexico, and
Arizona. The settlement in detail is left to you.
You will inform the President of the above most
secretly as soon as the outbreak of war with the
United States of America is certain and add the
suggestion that he should, on his own initiative,
invite Japan to immediate adherence and at the same
time mediate between Japan and ourselves. Please
call the President's attention to the fact that
the ruthless employment of our submarines now
offers the prospect of compelling England in a
few months to make peace." Signed, ZIMMERMANN.

The receipt of this information has so
greatly exercised the British Government that they
have lost no time in communicating it to me to
transmit to you, in order that our Government may
be able without delay to make such disposition as

may

1. Germany was going to start unrestricted submarine warfare (they were to sink passenger ships as well as American battleships) on February 1, 1917.
2. Germany wanted Mexico to go to war against the United States.
3. Germany offered to give U.S. territory—Texas, New Mexico, and Arizona—to Mexico in return for Mexico's support.
4. Germany expected to force Great Britain to sign a peace treaty because German submarines were sinking so many British ships.

You could use the Zimmermann telegram in any of the following ways in a class report:

- Find Germany, Japan, Mexico, and the southwestern states mentioned in the telegram on maps.
- Read about the British efforts to crack the code used in the telegram.
- Find out what else was happening in the United States from 1916 to 1918 that influenced Americans' feelings about World War I.
- Think about why Mexico might want the Southwest territory. How much would it extend Mexico's borders? What former disputes over this territory did the United States and Mexico have?
- Look at newspapers published during World War I. Find out what Americans said about the Zimmermann telegram. Add these quotes to your report.
- Find other documents that changed the course of history. (You might look up the message wrapped around a cigar before the battle of Antietam in the Civil War, the Monroe Doctrine, the breaking of the Japanese codes during World War II, or the transcripts from the Watergate trials.)

Census Reports

In 1835 the U.S. government required the Office of Indian Affairs to conduct a census (a count) of the Cherokee Indians. On page 44 is a copy of one of the pages of the report, which was done to determine the value of Cherokee land and to count the actual number of Cherokees living on it.

The census report is in the form of a chart. Reading a chart to find specific information is a skill which can be learned and applied to other documents. How do you develop this skill?

- First ask yourself, What does the title of the chart tell me?
- Second, look at each category as if it were a title; ask what is being discussed or listed?
- Decide what other skills, such as map reading, math, science, or decoding, can help you find the information you are seeking.
- What other primary sources can help you understand this chart better?
- Is there another way to organize the information?
- Is the information on the chart sufficient or will you need to research other documents and books?

Look carefully at the chart on page 44 to see if the following statements about the Cherokees are true.

1. Cherokee Indians farmed the land.
2. Some Cherokees owned slaves.
3. Corn was the most important crop.
4. Cherokees are listed in the census by their Indian names.

49

CENSUS OF CHEROKEES in the limits of *Georgia* in 1835,

HEADS OF FAMILIES, INDIANS, HALF-BREEDS, QUADROONS, AND WHITES.	RESIDENCE, STATE AND COUNTY, AND WATERCOURSE.	MALES Under 18 yrs.	Over 18 yrs.	FEMALES Under 18 yrs.	Over 18 yrs.	Total Cherokees.	SLAVES Males.	Females.	Total Slaves.	Whites connected by marriage.	Farms.	Acres in cultivation.	Houses.	Bushels wheat raised.	Bushels corn raised.	Bushels corn sold.	Fur tree mark.	Bushels corn bought.	Fur tree mark.
Eulaulanah	Floyd County, Etowah Clower's River	6	1	2	3	12					1	6	2		10	31		30	15
The Spirit	"	1	1	6	2	10					1	5	1		1			25	12½
Nancy Harris	"	1	4	3	2	10					1	12	3		80			12	12
John Fields	"	8	8	3	1	10		1	1		1	20	9		160				
Stitch	"	1	2	3	4	10					1	5	3		100				
Sucking	"		1		1	2					1	2	1		30				
...																			
		70	68	76	78	292	22	19	41	3	42	769	172	11	4035	3060			103	574

A census of the Cherokee Indian population in 1835

Other Legal Documents:
Ship's Manifest

The final document we will examine in this chapter is a ship's manifest from 1847. A manifest is a list of passengers or freight carried on board ship. The captain is always required to submit this list to Customs when the ship docks. Manifests might contain information about the age, sex, nationality, and destination of each passenger.

Choose one individual listed on the manifest and try to reconstruct the life of that person from the information given. Take Amy Brogan, for example. She is a twenty-one-year-old servant from Ireland who came to America in May 1847. Now try another name, Pat Murphy. Can you identify his age, occupation, nationality, and destination? Is he going to Canada or to the United States?

Think of the ways in which you can use this information to explain a theory or support an idea. Interpreting facts is a useful skill. If you take the known facts about Pat Murphy, for example, and draw some conclusions, you are interpreting information that will help you discover more about the times in which he lived.

Asking questions is a good way to begin. Why did Pat Murphy leave Ireland? What was happening in Ireland at that time that would make him want to leave his home? Did you notice that the names of many of the passengers are Irish? Find out what life was like in Ireland in the late 1840s.

- Where was Pat Murphy going? Can you think of reasons why he might have wanted to come to America?

- How do you think Americans felt about Irish immigrants coming to the United States?

NAMES.	AGE.	SEX.	Occu[pation]
Mrs Susan McLane	30	female	
Miss Isabella McTremlett	18	"	
Louisa A Tremlett	30	"	
Mr. B C Brehm	36	Male	M[ ]
Wm Mowat	25	"	Ca[ ]
Revd Peter Ross	38	"	
Cath McAntosh	20	female	
Mary Byrne	40	"	Ste[ ]
Mary Byrne	19	"	
Cath Welsh	21	"	Dr[ ]
Mary Ann Fuzzle	17	"	
Ellen Flenn	32	"	
Mary Mackie	53	"	Ste[ ]
Sarah McGlinch	45	"	
Mary McGlinch	13	"	
Bridget McGlinch	7	"	
Ann McGlinch	1/10	"	
Amy Brogin	20	"	Ste[ ]
Katharine Dolin	24	"	
Mary Dolin	14 Mo	"	
Patt Murphy	30	Male	Tra[ ]
John Buckly	30	"	My[ ]
Danl McLeod	40	"	La[ ]
Edward O'Cond	40	"	[ ]
Michael Elward	32	"	La[ ]

Acadian ___ of _Boston_

157 ___ tons, and 95ths of a ton, bound from the Port

Country to which they severally belong.	Country of which they intend to become inhabitants.	Remarks relative to any who may have died or left the vessel during the voyage.
Nova Scotia	Nova Scotia	
New Foundland	"	
Nova Scotia	"	
Scotland	Canada	
U States	U States	
Nova Scotia	"	
"	"	
"	"	
"	"	
Ireland	"	
"	"	
"	"	
"	"	
"	"	
"	"	
"	"	
"	"	
"	"	
"	"	
"	"	
"	"	

- What might lead you to think that America's immigration laws were more open at this time? Why might America have needed more people?
- Was immigration at this time different from other periods of American history?

After you have answered all your questions, you can then draw some conclusions about life in Ireland in 1847. These conclusions might explain why Pat Murphy and others listed on the manifest came to the United States and Canada. If Pat Murphy or another passenger had been one of your ancestors, you might be able to explain why he or she came to America and started the American branch of your family tree.

5

Diaries
and Journals

Journals and diaries are much alike. Both are written personal records. A diary is a daily record of events, while a journal is more likely to be an account of events or periods written at various intervals. Historians use both diaries and journals as primary sources because they are firsthand records of the past.

Reading the actual words of someone who lived a long time ago can be exciting. In a sense you are holding a piece of history in your hands. *The Diary of Anne Frank,* for example, is the written record of the feelings of a young girl who had to live hidden in an attic during World War II. Reading her words today helps you understand the terrible deeds of the Nazis and what it was like to live under a totalitarian government.

Suppose you are going to write a report about why people immigrated to America and what life was like when they first settled here. What general statements might you be able to make about immigrants to our country from actual journal accounts?

You are about to read portions from two journals which were written by people who came to live in America. The journals have been reprinted exactly as they were originally written. Although the time periods are

You can read about the actual experiences and feelings of someone from the past in a diary or journal.

different, and the immigrants' experiences are not identical, you should be able to find evidence from each journal to support general statements such as the following:

1. People leave their homelands in search of better living conditions.
2. For many emigrants, America represented the land of opportunity.
3. Most immigrants were poor and barely able to afford the trip to America.
4. Families were often separated because there was not enough money for every family member to come to America at the same time.
5. The voyage to America was long and difficult.
6. Getting started in America was often difficult.
7. New immigrants tried to live near people with similar backgrounds.
8. Learning to speak English was important.
9. Immigrants helped other family members come to America and get started.

Read each journal and try to find the evidence to support the general statements above. If you were using these journals for a school report, you would write the supporting evidence under each general statement or write down the numbers of the paragraphs with the supporting evidence under each general statement.

When you finish reading, review the general statements and decide if they are valid, based on the material in the journals.

The journal of Charles J. Hoflund (1834–1914) recounts his journey from Sweden to America in 1850. He was fifteen years old when he sailed for America with his parents, brothers, and sisters. The voyage took eight weeks.

About this time [1850] quite a number of families had emigrated to America and had written back from time to time. These letters would circulate and be read until they were so soiled and worn that it was difficult to read them. I was the only one who could read these letters, and they seemed to have a marked effect on those who heard them, for they were the cause of a great number leaving and going to America. About this time I came across a little book which contained something about Indians and Niagara Falls. It was wonderfully interesting reading for me.

• • •

At this time we had two good horses and one good yoke of oxen, so we did considerable freighting during the winter, but for all that I thought I could see it was nip and tuck for us to hold our own, and when I cast my thoughts into the future to try and see what there was in store for me, I did not find the prospects very bright. Instead my future would be full of hard and gloomy struggles. I pictured to myself a little cot on some out of the way, lonely, gravel knoll, for which I would have to work a certain length of time before securing for myself. These thoughts and pictures occupied my mind not a little and did not contribute to a happy and contented life.

In the fall I was sent to do some plowing in a stubble field with a yoke of oxen, which was not an easy task for a lad of my age (I was fifteen that fall), as the ground was very stony, some large boulders on the surface and underneath would cause the plow handle to land in the stomach, which would get mighty sore after a few hard thumps. But I was getting along quite well for it was work that I liked, but all of a sudden I had an experience which is hard for me to describe, though I remember it as well as if it had happened yesterday. While I was working along, it seemed to me as though I was enveloped in a dark cloud, and such gloomy feelings that came over me have never been experienced before or since. It seemed to me it was a power from some source compelling me to quit my work. So resolving with all my might to take whatever consequences, but never to plow another furrow, I unhitched the oxen from the plow, went home, put the oxen in the barn, and then went into the house where mother was sitting at the loom weaving. I told her of my resolve never to go back to that field even if father whipped me blue.

"I will never go back, never, never, never."

Well, she commenced to cry and said: "Dear child, what is the matter with you"?

"Nothing, only I will never go back there to work as long as I live," and I never did, and furthermore, I was never asked to do so. That was the last plowing for me in Sweden. My next was in Clover Township, Henry County, Illinois, U. S. A.

Sometime after this father and mother began talking America. . . . but it was not a thing easily decided, for all that was known by the common people was what we had learned from the letters of those who had gone, and they contained much that was hard to believe. At this time but a very few had gone from our neighborhood, I believe one or two families, and they located near Andover, Henry County, Illinois. I remember reading the letters they sent their relatives, in which they made a statement of how many pounds of pork a man was offered for a day's work, and it was nearly unbelievable to us peasants in Sweden that so much could be paid for one day's labor.

Finally, however, we decided once and for all to go to America. There were six children in the family, all rugged and healthy, but it required not a little resolution to overcome the difficulties, real and imaginery. For even if we succeeded in getting across, what would we find or what new trouble would be awaiting us? We had means enough to take us there, but very little more and this also worried us not a little. As soon as it was known that father had decided to go to America there was an onslaught from relatives and friends, begging and protesting with tears not to go, and picturing all manners and calamities to which we might be exposed. So it required a great deal of courage to give up what was considered a good thing for an uncertainty, to leave a place that had supported us and our forbears for generations, and not a kith or kin had ever left it for unknown and strange pastures. But from this time America was uppermost in our thoughts and conversation, and before winter was over two other families in our parish had decided to go along. Also father's sister and brother-in-law with their two children reached the same conclusion, and so it was quite a little company when we got together.

[53]

. . . Gottenberg, Sweden

We left on the 21st day of June, 1850. The following is a copy of the receipt we received from the ship company:

"Passage fare to New York, by the ship Virginia, Captain E. A. Jansson. I have this day received from landholder G. P. Hoflund, wife and six children, the sum amounting to 275 ricksdaler banco, which is hereby receipted."

Gottenberg, the 21st of June, 1850.

Olaf Wyke,
H. P. Matern.

On leaving we entered the ocean through Gottenberg harbor. We now depended upon the winds for our motive power to push us ahead, and everything went all right, although more or less fear possessed us. It had been rumored that the ship Virginia was condemned by the authorities as unseaworthy. It had plied between Gottenberg and New York for many years, but the captain they said was safe, and a good and careful man. As we passed on into the ocean, standing on deck I looked back and what a wonderful feeling arose with the thought that it was the last sight I would have of my native land. The horizon presented a blue line of rocks, with no trees to break the jagged outline. That was the last sight of land until we entered the harbor of New York, after one day less than two months of voyage and sky and water. It got to be pretty monotonous and some of us were sick all of the time. The only ones who were not sick was father and my youngest brother.

• • •

I was sick more or less all of the time for the two months, and what I lived on I can't imagine, for we had nothing much to eat. Father bought a lot of hardtack, what it was made of I don't know, but we didn't relish it to say the least. We had to get our own meals, but had no place to cook coffee or anything else.

When we came into port we began to realize that we were in a country where our language was no good to us. At that time there were very few Swedes in America. Father went ashore to see if he could find someone who could give us the information we needed. He was shown to Captain Erickson, who I think, was the same man who invented the famous Little Monitor that cut such a prominent figure in the Civil War. What little money we had had to be changed and we took a steamboat on the Hudson for Albany. I don't remember how long we stayed in New York City but it could not have been more than a day or two. When our things finally were carted over to the steamer and we had all gotten aboard we found that father was missing, and this, of course, caused a great deal of excitement. Mother and Aunt were nearly beside themselves, but just as the last bell was ringing he came poking along just in the nick of time.

Sometime in the evening we started for Albany and we had to huddle together as best we could on the deck. I remember peeping into the cabin on this boat, and to me it seemed as though a heaven had been opened. Next morning we arrived at Albany and there we were in for another change from the steamboat to a canal boat which was pulled along by horses on the shore. I have no recollection of how long it took us to travel from Albany to Buffalo, but I remember some of the experiences we had. The country looked good to us, and we were glad we were not on the ocean, but there was a great deal of sickness that made it unpleasant. Then we had no place to stay but down in the hull of the boat among the boxes and barrels, and we had hardly anything to live on. When we arrived at the locks some of the girls would leave the boat and go to a farmer's house and come back ladened with good things; cake and pie and bread and everything you can imagine and we would live high for a time. A good many complained of the bread tasting salty, but to me it was manna from heaven, for my stomach had had a long rest and anything tested fine.

From Buffalo we got a steamboat which was to land us in Chicago. We were favored with good weather on the Lakes, and if a wind should have come up I am sure we would have capsized, for the crew of the boat was kept busy nearly all of the time rolling scrap iron barrels from one side of the ship to the other in order to keep the proper balance. At times the boat would scuttle to one side and everyone was panic stricken.

When we arrived in Chicago we hunted up a family who had emigrated one year before and had settled in Chicago. Their name was Speake. How we found them I am at a loss to know, but I remember going there one afternoon. We crossed the Chicago river on a raft, since there were no bridges then as there are now. These people were distant relatives of ours and, like most of the emigrants, were very poor. Nevertheless, we were glad to be with someone who could talk with us and who had picked up a little knowledge of this country.

Father hired a team here to take us over the country to Andover, Henry County, Illinois. . . .

We loaded the wagon with sacks, trunks and bundles to its utmost capacity and all who were able had to walk, especially up-hill . . . We arrived there in the afternoon of the first day of October, 1850.

Andover was nothing but a name. Our freighter said, "here is Andover." On the south was the white oak grove, and in every other direction was the vast extending prairie. Father had expected to find something of a place, and he objected to being dumped off on the open prairie, but finally through a Swede, who happened to be working nearby, he learned that this spot was really Andover. We unloaded, and in the course of the afternoon we found a Swede widow-lady who lived nearby. . . . We were allowed to take our possessions into her yard, and there under the trees of the locust grove, we stayed all night.

The next morning, which was the first for me in Andover, a man came in and said he wanted a boy or young man to do some work for him on the farm. Someone pointed me out and the result was that I went with him. His name was Stoddard, and I worked with him about a year. I have reason to be thankful for this opportunity because I was in a good family and they treated me very fine. . . . Mr. Stoddard lived about four miles south of Andover in Oxford township. We arrived home about noon and after putting up the horses, we went in to dinner. That was the first time I had sat down to a spread table since we left Sweden, and was the first square meal I had had since we left.

But now I was brought up against the fact that I couldn't make myself understood. I realized now what it was to be in a foreign country and away from home. I had never been away from home in all my life before, and had scarcely even been away from my parents. I did not even know how to say "yes" or "no" in the language, and when the family tried to talk with me it made me terribly embarrassed. . . . Finally I made out that

[56]

they wanted to know whether I had any brothers or sisters, and I held up my fingers as a sign that I had five. After dinner Mr. Stoddard sent me with his two sons, both younger than I, to help herd some cattle which were feeding in a neighboring pasture. That was my first occupation in America. I made good use of these two boys that afternoon in trying to pick up some words. . . .

Hyman Wigodsky's journal tells about leaving Poland and coming to live in America in 1912. He was seventeen years old.

I was born, May 18th, 1894, in the city of Lodz, (Russian-Poland) I was one of five children, by my parents; David and Cipra Wigodsky. . . .

The people in Lodz and all over Poland were under constant pressure from the Russian government (the Czar's) especially the jewish people.

There were always uprisings of some sort. I must have been about four or five years old, when the Cossaks came into the city, one day with such a storm; it lasted two days. Those Cossaks were known as barbarians (killers). They were shooting at people on sight, even through the windows. . . .

I remember one particular night. My father made us sleep on the floor, directly under the windows, in order the bullets should not hit us. My younger brother Harry was so petrified and scared of the noise; he started to stuttering. (He is still affected from that incidence) . . .

They were poor at the time. My father was working in a Soap store, cutting and selling soap. He earned ten rubles (dollars) a week. We all lived in a two room appartment, (7 people). There were two beds and a table; (called Shlaban), this shlaban, was used for eating by day, and at night, it opened up like a bed, my three sisters slept in it. . . .

None of the children were old enough to work. My mother established a retail Vinegar business, in our appartment. She bought vinegar by the barrel, we all helped, filling the bottles and put labels on them. At first, we sold it to neighbors, later on; we hired a boy to deliver it to Grocery stores. But with five children, to take care of; was almost impossible, for my mother to keep it up.

My father, was forced to give up his job, to take over the Vinegar business. He bought a horse and wagon, on installment, also empty bottles, printed up labels etc., but the profits were so little; they could hardly get along. Eventually; they had to give it up.

Since my father was not successful in his business, he decided; to try his luck elsewhere. He went to Germany, by himself. He stayed there about two years, came back; very discouraged.

My mother wrote a letter, to her sister Gnendel, in America, asking her for help. My aunt sent two tickets, to come to America. Since my sister, Sarah, could not get along with Mother, or anybody; So, my Father decided to take her with him. But, it was not that easy, we had to trick her, we sent her to a fortune teller, to help her decide. (we tipped the fortune teller in advance) to tell her; that a wealthy man is waiting for her in America. Sarah fell for it, and went with my father to America. A fellow by the name of Morris Feivishevitz, who worked for my cousin, Schaya Eilenberg, in Lodz, went along with them. . . .

HOW I BECAME A PRINTER

Since my folks were in the vinegar business, they used to send me, to the printer, for the labels, to paste them on the bottles. One day, I asked Mr. Greenberg, the owner for a job. He hired me under the following conditions; in order to learn the trade, I had to work, one year without pay. Starting as an errand boy. The only money I earned; was tips, when I delivered orders, to customers. But, they taught me the printing trade; from A to Z. After the year was up; they paid me ten rubles (dollars) a MONTH.

Those years, the printing presses were driven by, foot-paddleing. My boss's wife wanted to reduce, so, she was standing next to me, helped me, by kicking the paddle. She also called me in the back of the print shop, to tighten her corset. After a while; I found a job, that paid me three and a half rubles a week. And I did not have to kick the paddle, with my foot, any more. The presses were running by electricity. I worked there, until I left for America.

CHAPTER III

In 1912, five months after my father was here, he sent us two more ship tickets, to join him. Now there was a problem again; my Mother was still left with four children. My mother refused to leave any one of us, behind. So, we decided; that my sister Gussie and I, should go first.

My sister and I, started our trip, the early part of December, 1912, a day before we left; all my friends, boys and girls, surprised me, with a Bon-Voyage Party, in my house. I found there; Arthur Strausbert (Strass) Sam Zitnitzky, Morris Rosen, Louis Kalish, Dincha Polansky and many others. They even performed a show, for us. "The Husband Under The Table". I can still remember; walking toward the train, my friends and relatives, walked along they noticed somehow; I felt sad leaving my Mother behind.

• • •

We finally got on the ship (Kronland), a Belgium ship. The first day I felt wonderful, I got aquainted with a nice girl, my age. We spent the whole day on deck together. The next day, and the rest of the trip, I was so sea-sick, I thought; I will never reach our destination.

We arrived into Ellis-Island, Wednesday, February Fifth, 1913, at 3 pm. My father was waiting for us, with my aunt Gnendel. They gave me a banana, (which I never saw that before) I honestly, did not know what to do with it.

My sister Gussie, was taken to another aunt Chana Edelman, to live there. My father took me to his home, which was; the back of that chocolate factory (where my father slept with that fellow Morris Feivishevitz) now that I took his part of the bed; Morris had to move.

After three months, that was in April; we sent for the rest of the family. We bought the ship-tickets, and some furniture, on installment, it took us about two years, until we paid everything off. My mother, my brother and sister Yetta, arrived just for Passover holidays.

6

Museums, Historic Sites, and Other Places of Interest

Museums and field trips—to an old gold mine, a power plant, or a historic site such as Edgar Allan Poe's home, for example—are excellent sources of information. In this chapter you will learn how to observe a museum's exhibit and come home with solid information. The skills you develop while visiting museums can also be used on tours.

It is often difficult to select what you think is important information and then remember it when you get home. You can avoid confusion by taking notes during your visit.

Asking yourself some questions as you look at various museum exhibits will enable you to focus your attention on finding the information you need.

- What is the title of the exhibit?
- What time period does the exhibit cover? Is this the time period I am interested in?
- What important places are shown in the exhibit? Are they locations I am researching?
- What important people are featured in the exhibit?
- What contribution did they make to American culture or history?

- What can I learn about the past from this exhibit? What can it tell me about the way people live now or may live in the future?
- How can I use this information in a report or project?

Very often a museum is so large it is overwhelming. How can I possibly take all this in? you might ask. How can I find what I'm looking for? Following a set of questions such as the one above will help you remember your purpose and offer you some guidelines.

Keep in mind that the museum curator (the person in charge of all or part of a museum) has arranged the exhibits in specific ways for a reason. Try to follow the exhibit in the correct order. Understanding the reason for the exhibit and its arrangement will help you digest the information.

MAKING
YOUR OWN MUSEUM

Have you been a member of a study group? Does the following conversation sound familiar?

"Do you understand what we have to do for this project?" asks a bewildered Ellen.

George offers, "We are supposed to show the rest of the class what we know about what life was like during World War I."

Take careful notes when you tour a museum or historic site.

"I hate oral reports. As for a slide show, there isn't enough time," says Martha.

Tyrone has the answer. "Why don't we make our own museum? I'd like to show what people wore, what houses were like then, and how people got around. We can even find pictures that show which members of our own families lived then."

If your group has to make a class presentation you might consider putting together your own museum. It is not difficult and it can be exciting. Decide what you will exhibit, collect the materials, label the items, plan the exhibit layout, and write explanations for each object in the museum. You might do the project about life during World War I. A social history project such as this one can inspire an endless number of fascinating exhibits.

Begin your exhibit with a display of pictures from this time period, showing the styles of dress and the way people traveled, worked, and played.

Another part of the exhibit could be objects and heirlooms of this era. Question family members about old school yearbooks or clothes and uniforms that may be stored away. Perhaps letters that your great-grandfather or great-grandmother wrote have been saved. Letters are primary sources which should be included in the museum.

At some stage in the preparation of the museum you may find it necessary to review your class notes to decide what should be included in the exhibit. A trip to the library can also generate new ideas or help you decide what to include.

Once you have collected enough material for your museum of life during World War I, you will be familiar with how people lived, how they felt about the war, and the problems they faced.

Arrange your exhibit by categories such as pictures, heirlooms, and perhaps even a time line. How will you present your museum to the class? Consider the amount

*This group put together their own museum exhibit
about life during World War I.*

of space you will have. You may need to hang clothing, uniforms, or family-tree charts on the walls. Separate tables can be used for each category of memorabilia. Be sure to label each display so that others can learn from your museum.

MUSEUM DISCOVERY BOX

Suppose your assignment is not part of a group project but an individual one. You can still make a very dramatic "museum" of your own, called a "Discovery Box Museum." Everything you collect about a certain time period is put in a box. Since you will be preparing an entire exhibit yourself, keep your topic narrow. Life in the 1920s may be suitable for a whole group to work on together, but one person should choose one segment of life in the twenties, like school life. You might choose to display school books of that time, class photographs, report cards, and graduation announcements.

In order to make a discovery box museum about school life in the 1920s, you need the following materials:

- a large clothing box
- a collection of photographs and other display items showing school activities
- a folder to display the pictures
- any background material, such as school books, report cards, or letters which will help your classmates understand what is being shown in the photographs
- a tape recorder and blank tape
- a written explanation of your display

- written directions on how to use the discovery box museum

Now set up the discovery box museum.

1. Display the photographs in order.
2. Explain the photographs in a written report.
3. Make a tape recording of the written report and place the tape and tape recorder in the box.
4. Number other primary-source materials and place them in the box. Make a key for these items so your classmates will know what they are.
5. Write directions on the cover of the box so your classmates can "visit" your museum and listen to your taped report on their own. Follow each step in your directions first, to make sure everything works as planned. Make any needed corrections before opening your unique museum to visitors.

The advantage the discovery box museum has over the group project is that it allows classmates to examine your collection at their leisure. It is also portable and can be used over again. It can even be displayed in the library.

Museum discovery boxes can be used by any classroom or club group. They are useful devices to introduce or review topics. They are an excellent way to use primary sources and share them with others.

TAKING A TOUR

All year tourists line up to tour the White House. If you were making this tour, you might find that your notes would be brief, similar to the ones on the next page.

Notes on my White House Tour:

Got in line 10:00 A.M. Waited 25 minutes to go in.

Entered through the East Wing.

Saw library, china room—both roped off so visitors only
look in. So much silver!

Upstairs to East Room. It's huge! Much larger than it
looks on TV. In this room—press briefings and bill
signing.

Saw Red room, Green room, Blue room.

Dining room—very grand.

Art—especially liked pictures by Audubon and Washington portrait saved by Dolly Madison.

Important home of all U.S. presidents, except George
Washington. It wasn't built when he was president.

Tour guides are secret service agents who are specially
trained for White House duty.

INCORPORATING YOUR INFORMATION
INTO A REPORT

Taking notes will help you remember what you saw and
enable you to write a summary of your White House
tour. Summaries can be used in several ways. For example, to summarize what you learned from reading the two
journals in chapter 5, you could write a short introduction that states the authors' names and the important
dates. Then you could list such information as where
each young man came from, how they both found work
in America, and the difficulties they faced in a new land.
Finally, a summary of this type could include your reac-
tions to the journals and your evaluation of the material
as a primary source of information.

Another kind of summary could be based on the notes you took on a field trip or a tour of an important building like the White House. Such a summary might look like this one.

After waiting in line to see the home of the presidents of the United States, I found myself in the East Wing of the White House looking at the library and china room. The china room is not large, but it is filled with expensive and beautiful bowls and art objects. Visitors are not allowed in the room, but I enjoyed what I could see from the doorway.

Upstairs we saw portraits of famous Americans and many rooms that are named after the color of the furniture and wallpaper. The East Room was fun to be in because I've seen it on television when the president has a press conference. It looked empty without all the newspaper reporters. The president signs many bills in this room. These bills then become our laws.

My favorite picture is the one of George Washington that Dolly Madison saved when the White House was burned down in the War of 1812.

I enjoyed the tour and found out a lot of information about this building. I thought the most unusual fact is that President Washington never lived in the White House.

Summarizing is a skill that can help you remember important information as well as organize it into a report that can be easily read and understood. The following steps can help you write good summaries:

1. Make certain that you understand all the information you have collected and have written down all important facts.

2. Arrange all your facts in a sensible order—chronologically or by importance or interest.

3. When you are summarizing information from notes, remember that you may not need to include everything you have jotted down. Use only the information that is related to your paper or project.

A summary is a useful way to organize ideas in your own mind and make them clear to others. Your ideas will be clear if you stick to your topic (what you saw on the tour, for example), and use a lot of details, and link those details together in a logical order. You will write good summaries if you are careful to follow these steps:

1. Make sure you supply enough specific and concrete details to show exactly what you observed.

2. Think through your subject matter before you start writing. This will help you include only relevant material.

3. Present your ideas in an order that makes it easy for someone else to follow. Be prepared to write several drafts of your summary before you are satisfied that you are presenting exactly what you want to say.

7

Careers that Use Primary Sources

B y now you may be asking yourself, Can knowing about primary sources and how to use them help me get a job? The skills that you have learned about in this book are skills that most employers value. Some careers involve extensive use of primary sources. A brief look at a few of these careers will help you discover where your own interests lie.

WHO USES
PRIMARY SOURCES?

Archaeologists. In the field of archaeology, scientists look for and study the remains of past civilizations. Among their many responsibilities, archaeologists must be able to identify and date these artifacts, or primary sources, which are sent back to museums or universities for further study.

Archivists. These specialists collect, catalog, and restore valuable historic documents. Our National Archives in Washington, D.C. keeps important letters and papers related to our country's history. Also kept here are letters written to government officials. The original Constitution and Declaration of Independence are kept in the National Archives.

Anthropologists. These men and women study how people lived in past times and the relationship of their remains to their way of life.

Writers, Moviemakers, Actors, and Composers. Writing about a particular person or period in history requires accurate and interesting information. Primary sources can add authenticity and color to a story, play, movie, or piece of music.

Teachers, Historians, Scientists, Geographers, and Lawyers. Each of these professions relies on firsthand material.

Reporters and Journalists. Reporting an event accurately requires using an eyewitness' actual words or facts gathered at the scene.

CASE STUDY:
LAW ENFORCEMENT AND
PRIMARY SOURCES

Primary sources are of the utmost importance in police work. Police officers are trained to look for three kinds of primary sources:

1. Eyewitnesses
2. Information from victims
3. Physical evidence

An eyewitness is someone who has seen an event, such as a crime. Police officers are trained to question eyewitnesses and to evaluate their answers. Eyewitnesses must be isolated so that they will not be influenced by what others say about the event.

Police officers find it helpful to ask simple questions that do not influence peoples' answers, such as What color was the car? rather than a more leading question, Was it a dark car? They must word their questions carefully. For example, a short witness might think the criminal was tall. In this case, officers might ask the witness if the criminal was as tall as himself. Officers also take into account the type of work a witness does. For example, a car salesman might give a very accurate description of the suspect's getaway car whereas a witness who does not own a car might be unable to describe the car at all.

Police officers must be aware of the physical and mental condition of the victim because an agitated state of mind or a physical handicap could alter recollections. A victim may not be an eyewitness. An attack may have come from behind or the victim may have kept his eyes on the attacker's gun throughout his ordeal. Perhaps the victim has something to hide. For example, the victim might have lost money in a robbery and claim the amount was larger than it actually was. Police therefore must look at a victim's situation, too.

Physical evidence found at the scene of a crime is an important primary source that can help police find the criminal. The evidence must be protected until members of the special evidence processing branch of the police department can arrive and seal off the area. Police officers must be able to determine if the crime calls for such evidence processing and must make split-second decisions about the condition of the evidence.

The specialists who collect and process evidence are highly trained and skilled technicians, often from scientific or medical fields. They are skilled in recognizing and using primary sources as evidence. The technicians who gather and process evidence are not necessarily police officers. They are forensic experts trained to recognize and use primary sources to solve crimes. People who find such work interesting must have the following skills and interests.

Skills:

Cataloging

Precision and accuracy

The ability to draw conclusions from information and facts

Well organized

Interests:

Math

Law

Medicine

Computer technology

Can you think of ways in which your own special interests match the skills needed for the careers you have learned about in this chapter? Remember that the skills involved in using primary sources are skills you will use all your life. Knowing how to use primary sources can help you make decisions in your everyday life and form opinions after carefully examining the facts in any situation.

For Further Reading

This list will help you find out more about the kinds of primary sources mentioned in this book. Those marked with an asterisk are novels in which primary sources (diaries, letters, artifacts, and memorabilia) play a vital part. We hope that the following suggestions will lead you to many other good books.

*Blos, Joan W. *A Gathering of Days. A New England Girl's Journal 1830–32.* New York: Charles Scribner's Sons, 1979.
   (A thirteen-year-old girl's experiences of life in New England.)

*Clements, Bruce. *Prison Window, Jerusalem Blue.* New York: Farrar, Straus, and Giroux, 1977.
   (An English brother and sister are captured and taken as slaves by Vikings in the ninth century.)

Dawson, Sarah Morgan. *A Confederate Girl's Diary.* Bloomington, IN: Indiana University Press, 1960.
   (This diary reveals what life was like for those caught up in the tragic events of the Civil War.)

*Field, Rachel. *Hitty Her First Hundred Years.* New York: Macmillan, 1929.

(Although written over fifty years ago, these fictional memoirs of a doll carved from wood are so entertaining that they span the decades.)

Frank, Anne. *Diary of a Young Girl*. New York: Doubleday, 1967.

*Glaser, Dianne. *The Diary of Trilky Frost*. New York: Holliday House, 1976.
(Life in a log cabin during the early 1900s.)

Hartley, William G. *Preparing a Personal History*. Salt Lake City, UT: Primer Publications.

Hoops, Roy. *The Home Front*. New York: Hawthorn Books, 1977.
(Interviews with people who lived in America during World War II.)

Luce, Iris, ed. *Letters from the Peace Corps*. Washington, D.C.: Robert B. Luce, 1964.
(Eyewitness accounts and letters of volunteers' experiences covering nearly every aspect of Peace Corps life in countries around the world.)

Meltzer, Milton. *In Their Own Words: A History of the American Negro*. New York: Thomas Y. Crowell, Vol. I, 1964; Vol II, 1965; Vol. III, 1967. (Three books covering the years 1619–1865; 1865–1916; 1916–1962.)
(The life of the American Negro from the arrival of the first Blacks in 1619 to the mid-1960s. The primary sources include letters, diaries, journals, autobiographies, speeches, newspapers, testimony given by Blacks when they appeared as witnesses before investigating committees of Congress and in public hearings, and other eyewitness accounts.)

*Park, Ruth. *Playing Beatie Bow*. New York: Atheneum, 1982.
  (Through the primary source of a lace collar, a fourteen-year-old girl learns about people and life in Sydney, Australia, a century ago.)

Shumway, Gary L. and William G. Hartley. *An Oral History Primer*. Salt Lake City, UT: Primer Publications.

Sloane, Eric. *Diary of an Early American Boy: Noah Blake, 1805*. New York: Funk and Wagnall, 1962.
  (Based upon a small, leather-bound diary written in 1805 and found in an old house. Included are many drawings of original farm tools.)

Terkel, Studs. *Hard Times: An Oral History of the Great Depression*, New York: Pantheon Books, 1970.
  (Interviews with people who lived in America during the Great Depression of the 1930s.)

*Watson, Jane. *The Case of the Vanishing Spaceships*. New York: Coward, McCann and Geoghegan, 1982.
  (This science fiction story tells of primary sources used to find a UFO.)

Weitzman, David. *My Backyard History Book*. Boston, MA: Little, Brown, 1975.
  (Projects and activities about the past to do with your family.)

*Westfall, Robert. *The Machine Gunners*. New York: Greenwillow Books, 1976.
  (Set during World War II, this is a story of an English boy and his friends who collect memorabilia of German soldiers.)

*Wiseman, David. *Jeremy Visick*. Boston, MA: Houghton Mifflin, 1981.
(A gripping historical fantasy that involves two boys, one living and one dead for over one hundred years, a gravestone, mining company reports, a chunk of copper, an old homestead, and an old mine.)

Index

About
the Authors

Helen H. Carey is senior editor/coordinator of the Project for an Energy-Enriched Curriculum for the National Science Teachers Association (NSTA). She was a teacher in the Prince Georges County school system in Maryland for twenty years. In 1974 she was named Outstanding Secondary Educator of America. Helen Carey lives in Adelphi, Maryland.

Judith E. Greenberg, a part-time teacher and educational consultant, taught social studies at the junior high school level for seven years. She lives in Potomac, Maryland.

907
CAR
   Carey, Helen H.
   How to use primary
   sources

DATE DUE			

726